Lavender Love Notes

Lavender Love Notes

Samira Vivette

Chapter illustrations by Allexis Varelle
ISBN: 978-0-6451638-0-3

To those needing some gentle reassurance,
I hope these pages help you see your uniqueness

There are times when all we need is a warm hug. And I don't purely mean a physical one. Seeking comfort in the form of movies, music, books, and food brings us peace because it is those shared experiences that bond us as human beings. It's the universal need to be understood, valued, and helped. The reassurance that someone before us has been there and come out stronger than before.

I like to think of this book as the little sister of *Pastel Dreams and Glittered Hearts,* infused with a calming aura in the shade of light purple. I wish for these words to be a beacon of hope, a pillar of strength, a reality check, a supportive friend. Within these pages especially, I wanted to replicate that feeling of drinking a hot cup of tea on a cold day, the feeling of your skin melting under a steaming hot faucet. Let my words be the advice from your best friend, the hug from a close relative. Let them be the compliment you receive from a stranger that leaves a smile on your face for the rest of the day. Allow these shared experiences and words of motivation to enlighten your wondrous soul, lifting you up and awakening the strength you've always longed for.

Love yourself while you struggle.
Love yourself through the grief.
Love yourself as you learn.
Love yourself and believe.

Love yourself with everything that you are during each stage of your rebirth, during each stage of rediscovering yourself. Delve into my soft-spoken lavender love notes for the ignition of the ultimate feeling: hope.

Walk with me through this rhyming journey of poems, prose, and letters to ourselves, our fears, and those feelings we wish we could personally address.

Self-love can feel like a challenge, especially during those times when we feel like we have failed or when others create ideals that can never be attained. But your passion has always lived within you. A power that might have been suppressed or ignored for far too long. In a world that primarily focuses on negativity, breathe, take a break with me, and reflect on the infinite nature of your capabilities.

Loving yourself is quite easy when everything is going your way, but it takes a perspective shift to practice self-care when things are going astray.

Unapologetically being content in your skin is the least you deserve. I hope you see yourself differently after the final page is turned.

Lots of Love,

Samira

Love Notes

Love yourself
while you
struggle

The struggle is inevitable.

You've heard it a million times in pop culture: the strength that is supposed to arise after conquering your fears, how victory has a smell when it is near. You have yet to feel this, no matter how many people tell you it exists, so you keep going, and going, and going until your soul bleeds. You keep crawling for that light at the end of the tunnel among shards of glass and impossibly heavy rubble. You persevere because of what others assure you, but you don't know if their words are genuine or a recycled version of someone else's story.

Still despite the uncertainty, you decide to keep going anyway because the risk of not listening seems far too great.

And you end up hating yourself when that goal drifts further away.

That goal might not seem any closer today,
But I promise you, it is within reach.
You just have to believe.
Like the downpour of rain when you are thirsty and weak,
This light at the end of the tunnel will appear
Sooner than you think.

One day,

The ache in your bones when you stand straight will dissipate.

The proudness of your accomplishments will resonate.

One day, darling,

You will be what you always hoped to see.

Feel your body become one with the wind. Visualize the weight of your worries patter down like raindrops falling onto a thousand leaves. Your soul is soaring at its own pace through the clouds above, carrying with it an abundance of harmony and love.

Your growth is being guided by the elements of nature.
This feeling of weightlessness, it can exist forever if you allow it.

grow your wings, darling

You must be gentle with yourself while you struggle. You are the wax dripping from the candle. You are the foam floating on the waves before they melt into the sand. You are the soft edges of a feather, the smooth feeling of untouched leather. But darling, you are also the wax when it hardens, the waves when they crash; you are the quill bleeding ink, the ruthlessness of hot leather when it burns skin. You are never given anything you cannot handle, so trust in the process and learn to let go. Believe in your resilience which sparkles in the millions. You are equipped with the ability to make it through anything. Your innate strength will transpire in the long run; and underneath the debris is a pair of wings ready to lift you up.

Some things you must leave
with the caring arms of the
Universe for she knows the
best way to go.

today is the day

I reassure my aching bones;
Today is the day I am kind to myself.
I wipe my tears with my jumper sleeve
And curl up into a ball.
Today is the day
I forgive myself.
It's about time
I kissed the wound
After I fell.

It's important to love yourself on your bad days more than anything. Stir in the sugar with even more delicacy than you would before. Allow your body to melt into the mattress and exhale those heavy thoughts. Close your eyes and wander to a place where you may soar above the mountains and swim with dolphins through underwater caves. Treat your soul as the visitor of this body of yours and try your best to make it feel at home. Be soft and mindful of your feelings, and give yourself plenty of time to heal alone.

That beaming smile
With wondrous eyes
Still lives inside,
Even on those days
When you feel like this world
Is robbing you
Of your life.

the number one

Believe in the power of the number one.
It takes one loose leg in the ladder to fall,
One bug in your shoe to make your skin crawl,
One bite of a new food to make you crave more,
One word to break a heart like it never existed at all.
But it also takes one person to give you a chance
You never thought you'd get
Which triggers a chain reaction
To guide you toward success.
All it takes is one small flame
Dancing on the wick of the candle
To bring hope to darkness
That feels impenetrable.
It only takes one moment in time
When fate is on your side
For the stars in the Universe
To perfectly align.

Keep hanging on for that number one
Because its power is underestimated:
That one person, that one moment,
That one lapse in judgement.
These are all little signs
That you are being guided
Towards the path
You are meant to be on.

What motivates you to get out of bed? Is it the screeching sound of your morning alarm, the blue light reflecting on the surface of your eyes? Is it the morning sun peeking through the blinds? The need to take your vitamins before your daily dose of exercise? Or is it that undying hunger to prove everyone wrong? To leave their opinions in the dust to become that person you always knew you were all along? Is the very thing that motivates you the thing they tried to suppress for so long? Tell me, is the fire within you so wild that it's burning all their tongues?

Enthusiasm is a beautiful trait. You must not lose it. I know it can be difficult maintaining a positive demeanor sometimes, and you cannot be blamed for seeing the world through a murky lens. But the choices that you make from now on are in your control. You are allowed to be upset for a long time; you are allowed to grieve. There is no rule to say you must bounce back like nothing happened, especially following a difficult period. You are hurting. Your essence is devoid of light. It is not reasonable to expect the emergence of a colorful aura shortly after you have been broken and left to die. Use this time to let the hurt seep from your bones. Allow the toxicity to bleed from your soul. This process is one that cannot be altered or sped up, contrary to what we have been told. You need to sit with all your emotions: the good, the bad, and the in-between until you find peace. Or that is, until peace finds you and wraps itself around your heart until you no longer feel incomplete.

You have carried the weight of your mind all these years.
Your spine is stronger than you think.

Dear Tender Ego,

They might be projecting their insecurities onto you but that is not your fault. Their actions may seem like they are deeply personal towards the essence of your being but I promise they have nothing to do with you at all. Their harsh words are not related to what they think of you but rather what these people think of themselves. Please understand this. What you have allowed them to see has only scratched the surface of the inner workings of your mind. And it is because of this fact, you should leave their surface-level comments behind.

Let the tears fall where they may.
It doesn't mean you are weak.
It doesn't mean they are here to stay.
These droplets only indicate
That you had a tough day,
But like everything in this world,
This sadness you feel
Is reassuringly
Temporary.

Some days,
I'll wake up with an
Unwavering excitement for life.
I'll draw the blinds and sit outside,
Sipping my tea contently at sunrise.

And some days,
The energy I so desperately need
Will cease to exist,
Leaving me unable to move my body
From underneath the sheets.

In these moments, I must remind myself
This life is all about contrast,
About the highs and the lows.
I need to bask in those days
When my body is tired
Just as much as those days
When I am on a high
Because to feel something is
To be alive
Even if I am not able
To control the tide.

Your lungs will function normally one day soon;
Your smile will defrost, and your heart will soften
After what seems like an eternity of doom.

Your body will flourish,
And you will return to normal,
Except the only thing
That will be different is
You will be stronger.

Remember this: you will never struggle in vain. Everything you have been through is to teach you a lesson far greater than you could comprehend. It is all part of a better plan.

These obstacles appearing on your path
Are simply a test to your strength.
Do not let them
Chip away
At your soul –
Instead, let them serve as motivation
To break them
At their very core.

marathons, cocktails, and tinted glasses

Can you see those people at the finish line?
They sit with smirks on their faces, sipping cocktails in every flavor.
They are crossing their fingers and placing bets not in your favor.

They don't care to see you win.
They do not want to see you finish the race.
They would rather see you break an ankle
Than achieve first, second, or third place.

They don't believe that final line will be crossed by your feet.
Their screams of encouragement ring loudest for your sworn enemy.
They sit on their chairs thinking they could do better,
Lying to themselves because they have nothing else to offer.

What you need to do is find that power within you:
The blaze from a dragon's mouth that annihilates everything in sight.
You must harness the fiery nature of your determination to fight.
Channel the strength of breaking the ground
With a superpower newly found.
Be merciless like acid rain about to come pouring down.

You will keep running.
Your feet will touch the finish line.
And you will feel that pain along the way
With the sweeter taste of victory
Forever on your tongue.

Grit your teeth
Through it.

The reward
Will be worth it.

dormant but dangerous

You are the dormant volcano
Surrounded by shark-infested waters
That everyone thinks is harmless for now
While living in denial of its eventual explosion.
They mistake your calmness for weakness –
Enough so to trample on your land
With a false sense of security,
But little do they know
The danger that awaits
If they were to be there
At the wrong time one day.
Your tenacity is ruthless and destructive,
Capable of eradicating anything in its path with ease.
They are under the assumption
That dormant means weak
When it really is to be
Quietly catastrophic.

It may feel self-righteous to fight for your body, your mind, your soul, to place undying confidence in your abilities, but this should be the norm. It should be the outsiders trying to convince you of what you lack, and it should be your self-esteem that always fights back. You should be the resistance to an invader's attack. An ally made of steel that holds up a frail back. Your confidence should serve as a bulletproof wall to their nasty opinions, blocking their attempts to shatter you and taint your talents. And so, you must keep fighting and fighting until their bullets run out because nobody can break your resilience now; your self-worth is too loud.

Never underestimate the power of the broken spirit.
Nothing comes back with more strength.

Some days, I can jump out of bed with a passion so strong that it makes me forget about the nightmare I just had. Some days, I'll wake up with eyelids stuck together because I spent hours the night before crying into my pillow and rubbing my eyes until I saw stars. Some days, it feels my body is functioning out of obligation and not because it yearns to thrive. Sometimes, it all hurts. A little too much. I appreciate you, my tired body. I still love you. I will still try my best to eat the foods you crave and sit on the floor of the hot shower for as long as you need to feel okay. I will appreciate you when you surprise me with your capabilities but also the times when you find it hard to breathe. My tired body, you are not any less useful on those days you struggle. My tired body, I am learning to love you on those days when society tells me you are nothing.

slow down

Remove the word "quit" from your vocabulary
And replace it with rest:
A hopeful four-letter word
Which tells the world you are not giving up,
But you are taking a break.

You are only human.
Your energy needs healing.
You are in the midst of recharging
Like a bear in hibernation
Or a lizard on the warm concrete.

Your desire for success may be insatiable,
But the health of your soul is non-negotiable.
Breathe in and exhale;
You are not under attack.
The world will still be waiting for you
After you relax.

This treacherous climb is not forever.
Please remember.

gentle heart

Those words you hesitate to speak about someone else
Are ones you mercilessly use to hurt yourself.
You must refrain from the small phrases
That you think don't matter
Because they will swell like a snowball
Tumbling down the mountain.

Speak with tones of lavender under your tongue,
And hug yourself with the warmth of a knitted scarf.
Become the tranquility of a salt-infused bath,
The innocence of a child's laugh.
It's your turn, darling,
To speak to yourself with love.
It's finally your turn
To show yourself
You are enough.

By comparing yourself to others with envious eyes, you will never be satisfied. Everybody out there is struggling in some way: some are just better at hiding it than you think. There are people you don't speak to who look at your accomplishments in awe, and there are those who feel the need to overcompensate with theirs because they don't have that confidence anymore. Everyone is in the same boat, whether you believe it or not. Many people are going home and wishing they were something more. Be comfortable in your own skin. Be proud of your existence. Nurture your spirit and don't let them taint it. Nobody else has walked in your shoes, therefore nobody else's opinion should matter to you.

I know your heart feels so heavy
That it's about to fall out of your chest,
But if you don't hang on,
You'll never know the beauty
That's about to come next.

These dull aches that linger in your mental space should not exist a moment longer. Exhale their presence with conviction because they are not wanted. Relax your shoulders and feel the lightness of your limbs. Envision the evaporation of those heavy emotions within. Everything you give power to eventually has power over you. And if you're not careful, they will surely destroy you. The intensity of your feelings cannot be denied, but you can control the weight of these burdens in which you carry, where you let them reside. Your heart should be a sacred space for the butterflies in your conscience to fly, a place where suppressed anger goes to die. Observe your destructive thoughts carefully and make sure they are never invited in. You wouldn't give your enemy a seat at your table, so why should these thoughts be any different?

You are still human,
Even when your world is heavy with pain.
Be gentle.

Dear Nervous Soul,

Look around more. I know your shyness makes you feel like curling into a ball, whether you're walking in a park among strangers or trying to navigate crowds at the mall. You avoid looking at anyone while you drift in your lane with feelings of uncertainty when somebody looks your way. Ignite the feeling of curiosity once more. Don't you remember looking around as a child and absorbing the details of the world? Speaking to strangers without caring what they thought? Take in this vibrant realm around you that wishes to be seen. Don't be scared to look around and take in your surroundings. Look beside you at the traffic lights at the person with their music blaring. Wave at people you know without feeling nervous for staring. Smile. Be present. Melt into the moment. Never feel like you must shy away from existing.

If only you treated yourself like you would a newborn baby: with delicacy, with patience, with a nurturing love that is unconditional. If only you cradled your insecurities until the crying settled, before melting into the abyss of your greatest dreams. If only you realized the fragility of self-acceptance, compassion, and affection: the gifts we give to others before we give to ourselves, the emotions we project until eventually we have nothing left. Treat yourself accordingly, like your skin is paper-thin; please, be gentle with the inner child within.

You may feel comforted by movie marathons and chocolate muffins or staying up and drawing until three o'clock in the morning. Do what makes you feel less numb to keep your soul alive; the healing will follow in time. Don't feel guilty for booking those fancy massages and yoga classes. Don't check your bank account after splurging on clothes that make you feel happy. Do not feel guilty for indulging in one too many glasses of wine and do not feel guilty for drinking them until you feel fine. These small indulgences have not gone in vain; they have simply helped keep you alive. This process, it will hurt. It is meant to. You will not know serenity unless you have felt earth-shattering pain. Contrast is necessary, and the peace you seek will blossom as a result of your survival. Keep hanging on for the moment it all comes together for you will thrive like you never have before. That moment is right around the corner.

You know the indescribable thirst-quenching feeling of drinking iced water on a scorching day?

That is how accomplishment tastes.

Stay consistent.
Remain vigilant.
Keep moving forward
With your unbreakable vision.

The greatest power you have
Is the fact you have been to hell and back.
The greatest assurance of your strength
Is your refusal to sit on the fence
Because you held that chain between your fingers
Until blood stained your skin.

You carried burdens so heavy,
They almost broke your back.

You survived that.

If you think some loose dirt on the mountain is
going to stop me from reaching its heights then
you definitely don't understand my will to climb.

You will find the more you speak about how hard something is, the more difficult it is to get back on track. Telling your mind what your body feels is a sure-fire way to convince you of what you lack. Your mind is the most powerful asset you have and your thoughts are the most destructive weapon against that. Be careful of those doubts that cross your mind because as harmless as they might seem, they can make or break your fight.

The amazement that flourishes after a silent achiever breaks their silence is nothing like you have ever experienced.

Struggle, darling,
This is an inevitable feat,
One that may wring your bones
Through the washer of defeat.
But reward, my darling,
Will surely follow
Because there is always
That light
At the end of the tunnel.

Your nerves are stinging right now, but you will heal again. Let these aches and pains have their moment. Let it burn. Let it hurt. Let the small shocks of discomfort fuel your spirit into fighting once more. Nobody gets to have the satisfaction of bringing you down. Nobody gets to feel too comfortable when you are around. The blood, these bruises, they are necessary steps in your healing. Allow the air to dry your wounds, and soldier on. You are not about to let your entire body down because of an uncomfortable cut on your arm.

Scream if you have to.

Punch walls if you need to.

Tense your body

And grit your teeth

Like you're about to

Plunge into the waters of the Arctic.

Do whatever you need

To make it out the other end.

But don't give up.

Don't you dare think about it.

They talk about victory being the sweetest thing you'll taste, so if you give up now, the only thing left on your tongue will be the taste of pain.

You're almost there.
These short breaths,
These aches in your bones,
These are temporary discomforts
To tempt you into giving up.

What will distinguish you
From the ones who get left behind is
You were willing to clench your teeth
Despite your body almost caving in;
You promised to see it through
Until the very end.

So keep fighting until your last breath.

They threw you to
the sharks hoping
you would die,
wildly unaware
that you were a
siren in disguise.

If you let them see you bleed,
You're going to have to let them
See you succeed.

victory

I know it's hard.
I know you feel like
You have been ripped apart.
But if you give up now,
How will you witness
The greatness to follow?
If you give up now,
Can you tell them to eat their words?
If you give up now,
Can you go to sleep knowing
You tried your absolute best?
Can you say you kept going
Despite the doubts and lack of rest?

I know it's hard.
I know you feel like you're breaking in half.

But when the pain begins,
That's when the victory starts.

Love yourself
through the
grief

The world may feel a little too heavy sometimes.
Too heavy for you to cry.
Too heavy for you to smile.
Too heavy to make sense of your purpose
So you'll sit and stare at the sky for a while.
The world will sometimes feel too light
While everyone and everything passes you by.
You'll feel like a stranger in your own home,
The feeling of your soul turned into stone.

But the world, one day, will feel just right.
It will be the warmth of a parent tucking you in at night.
The earthly wonders will ignite that sparkle in your eyes,
And your aura will shine so unapologetically bright.
Right now, this world may feel like a weight
You will never leave behind,
But one day soon, everything will feel alright.

Just like the seasons change,
This ache will eventually dissipate.
You must have faith.

Dear Tired Eyes,

You have more days ahead of you than you realize. You have that moment awaiting you when you find out you've had a lucky streak even though you've never once won anything. You will have the privilege of being there for your friends and family when they feel weak, to be a beacon of hope in their time of need. You will experience those moments when something life-changing happens that you never could have envisaged, those times when a sign from the Universe picks you up when you feel the weakest. But you also have the small things to live for: the extra change you receive when buying a coffee, a compliment from a stranger in the club bathroom. You will have those moments when you receive some good news on the way home from a tiring day or when you are up with friends laughing about old memories late. No matter how hard it gets, there are those days to look forward to. And when those days peek into your life, which they will, you will appreciate the true value of never throwing the towel in.

come with me

Sadness may be an unwelcome visitor,
But why cannot sadness still bear witness
To the beauty you will experience?

Sadness can still tag along
When you're listening to your favorite song.
Sadness can sit on your shoulders
While you cook your favorite dish in the oven
Or run amuck in a playground like a kid once more.

Sadness does not need to leave your sight
For memories to be made,
For new sceneries to wash your eyes.
Sadness is still a companion
When you feel like the light
Is nowhere in sight.

Allow sadness to join you if you have no other choice
Because this heavy friend will one day be a thing of the past,
And you cannot allow these priceless memories to pass.

Each time you wish for the pain to subside,
You are holding that pain within your eyes
For the future version of yourself to cry.

So, it is best for you to let it hurt.
For now, darling, just let it hurt.

softened edges

They are no longer by your side. And at one point in time, without them you thought you'd die, yet here you are, doing what you can to survive. For some reason, certain memories are not as vibrant as you remembered them in the moment. There is something missing and you just can't seem to pinpoint it. You're running errands, tangled in demands and timelines when you are only one bad day away from losing your mind. You feel numb to the idea of them as if your imagination's been polluted with a poisonous concoction. Sometimes, you're drowning in feelings of distress, and other times, you're doing perfectly fine. But if only they knew how much you miss them. If only they knew how many things still remind you of them.

You may have found the strength to keep living, but it does not mean you love them any less. Do not feel guilty for not crying as much as you thought; don't feel guilty for not thinking about them as much anymore. Life catches up with all of us, and the ache naturally begins to fade. But this is not indicative of your adoration for them, nor does it signify their importance. These feelings of ease are a sign that their spirit has made a home within yours. This is why you no longer feel like you are grieving. This is why you feel no trace of healing.

There is solace to be found in knowing they will forever be with you every step of the way because they never left you in the first place.

Your lips have curved with gravity's pull for too long.
Sweetheart, you must not let sadness win.

Dear Pain,

I'm scared of what you do to my body. I'm scared of the potential
you hold to destroy me. I am trying to work with you by my side, but
on some days, it feels like I have let the enemy inside. I need to
remember that you do not exist to simply inflict grief but to teach me
the deepest of lessons I would not have otherwise experienced. I
need to remember that you are the dried blood that covers my
wound, the concealment of a scar with a vivacious tattoo. You serve
as a barrier to the other pain awaiting to enter my body; you exist to
numb me from events that have the capacity to end me. Each and
every day, I am learning to grow more comfortable with you by my
side for I know that each lesson learned is less time spent in the
firing line.

loved and lost

They say it's better to have loved and lost
Than never to have loved at all,
But I never understood how there could be a positive side
To collapsing on the bathroom floor.
I never could fathom the complacency implied
While clutching your chest in agony, wishing to die,
The myriad of restless nights,
The isolation from those closest in your life.

But then it occurred to me,
How special to feel a love so deeply
That the absence of it rips apart your organs
Mercilessly.
How cruel the thought of two extremes:
Loving intensely and melting into another's energy
Or becoming acquainted with suffering.

I guess now, the more I think about it,
I feel grateful to have felt a love so strong
Because it means I have loved.
Truly loved.
And that feeling, I know now,
Is better than never having felt it at all.

Samira Vivette

Isn't it ironic how grief can tear us apart at the seams but also make us feel complete?

Dear Sweltering Scars,

You still hurt. And I don't know why. It feels like nothing can rid me of your presence, not even time. Pain has become my identity, my friend. These scars show me just how close I was to the end. I am still learning to embrace these marks of courage for otherwise, I cannot live with myself. The flaming lines etched into my essence have transformed into visions I do not have the heart to revisit. But despite the torment, I am holding on for these calloused memories to welcome their healing as the warmth of this world strokes them with reassurance. I know that day will come. And these tender reminders that ignite the deepest agony within my heart will eventually be an ornament of the past.

If only sadness was like the rom-coms where after a few phases of ice-cream tubs and ugly cries, you move onto a period filled with nothing but smiles. Sadness follows you everywhere, even after you've healed. Years later, you'll come across something that reminds you of their memory. And you might not cry, but you'll feel a little more dead inside. It will be like scarred skin being stroked; you'll be slightly more sensitive than before. You'll grow to be terrified of forgetting the little things. There'll be nights when you're throwing up from agony in the bathroom sink. You will spend a big chunk of your life wondering why your wounds have not healed with time. You will be angry at yourself for not remembering more of them when they were alive. You will convince yourself you are fine, knees on the ground begging for it all to rewind.

But starting the healing process does not mean you miss them any less. Healing is feeling their presence in everything you do and being comforted by the fact they will forever be that warmth in your chest. Healing is watching the colors in the sunrise morph into their smile. Healing is knowing that sensitivity will linger for a while.

And it's okay. It's perfectly normal.
You are not alone.

You are allowed to move on without truly moving on.

Hold your own hand like you would a friend or someone else's.
Loving yourself is not embarrassing or selfish.

I hope you go to sleep tonight knowing you did the best you could today. I hope you lie in bed feeling thankful that you made it through another twenty-four hours with its own set of challenges. I hope you close your eyes reassured that even if you didn't do some of the things you wanted to, you're not less of a person. You're getting up each and every day, and you're trying. For that you are strong. And darling, there is always tomorrow.

You don't need to figure it all out now.
Empower your mind to silence the doubt.
Just for now, focus on living, breathing,
Being here in this body of yours,
And basking in the wonderment
Of the ever-changing seasons.
Take off your shoes
And let your feet sink into the earth;
Focus on the simplicity of this world.
Be present in this moment.
Be thankful for it all.

troubles and tea bubbles

One day, I sat on the porch
With swollen eyes and a throat that had ceased
From crying and sobbing, choking on my tears,
Pondering why this feeling had chosen me.
My partner, despite my broken state, chose to nourish me;
He gently brought me a cup of tea.
Floating on the surface of the water
Were three bubbles resting idly.
Shaking the mug gently, they did not pop.
I stared in wonderment
At something so insignificant –
A non-existent predicament
Infused my soul with such contentment.
I felt myself dreaming under a cloud of serenity
As I melted into my chair with a sense of ease.
I hadn't felt hopeful for most of my life,
But when these bubbles refused to leave my sight,
I witnessed the smallest stream of light;
And that was the moment I learned to be content
With this dark cloud looming over my mind.
I finally felt the impermanence of this emptiness
And the fact it would not remain indefinitely.
I finally knew that these little signs meant
That this sadness will not become me.

if you can't cry just yet

You must be gentle with yourself
Until your body decides it is time
For the hurt to leave through your eyes.

For now, you are allowed to be content with
Blank stares, steaming hot showers,
And resting on the floor for hours.

You must treat yourself tenderly
And with patience,
And part of this comes an understanding
That your body is not yet ready to feel happiness.

Allow the tears to fall
Whenever they are ready.
There is no time limit
For your healing journey.

Your mind is just as tender as your heart.
Please remember that.

cycles

This magnificent Universe will continue to flourish regardless of the hurt you're feeling or the lives you've lost. There is beauty and comfort in this simple fact for the rain will still come down like it did that one morning you were sitting with the love of your life drinking coffee on their porch. Summer will never fail to leave its temporary souvenirs on your skin, and Winter will forever force you indoors with too many blankets and cups of tea. You will encounter people that make you lose faith in humanity, but you'll also meet those who make you believe pure souls exist. The negative encounters might open old wounds for a while and they may bring painful memories you would rather ignore, but everything comes full circle in this world. And I promise that one day, you will smile as the rain caresses your face because those same droplets have already met you once before: that morning you were sitting with the love of your life drinking coffee on their porch.

The essence of fear
May be something you hold near,
But the hands of hope are ready
To catch all your tears.

they never left

You may have lost them,
But you will never be alone.
Their energy will always be
Entwined with yours.
The adventures you shared
Found a home within.
Their habits and their quirks
Are embedded in your skin.
They may not be with you physically,
But they are with you spiritually.
They are still around you
In the little things you do,
So when the breeze whispers,
Make sure to listen out for your name
Because they are here,
And they are calling for you.

Your heart will remember this pain
And it will teach you that
In the game of life,
There exists dry, thirsty, bumpy terrain,
But also, the beauty to follow
Of endless sunshine and a month's worth of rain.

Pain is mental just as it is physical. Some memories will ache a little too much on days you simply can't handle it. But sadness, it is a reminder that you have been lucky enough to love something with your whole heart. A reminder that the ones you lost also felt this love, even if at the time you didn't feel you showed them enough. I assure you; they felt your love. The energy that connects us flows through the skies, transcending limitations in day-to-day life. This stream of magic is unconfined. It floats between lands and across seas to spread its message to those living and deceased. You may have sacrificed a part of yourself for that one you held dearly, but this part of you will not remain empty. Darling, you are going to witness moments which nurture the jagged parts of your soul and you won't even notice them at first: the child who waves and smiles at you with glistening eyes at the grocery store. The compliment you receive on the street from a friendly stranger. Those times when the odds aren't in your favor but you manage to escape danger. There will be moments like a certain song playing on the radio while you're thinking of the one you lost. An unfamiliar face repeating habits nobody else but you could know. It will be the little things: those minuscule moments you'll only notice when you pause to reflect. They will add up. And they will slowly repair the loss in your soul because these beautiful, seemingly insignificant moments that come to you are a sign that the one you love is closer than you know.

When I reflect on those times sadness squeezed the life from my lungs, I also remember it is those very moments that I have overcome.

I've been there for those who weren't there for me. Been a shoulder for those who didn't deserve me. I've been strong for those who felt weak. I've been the listener for those who needed to speak. And when everybody leaves, I'll still be all of these things. I'll be all of these things for me, and only me.

i miss you

You were the best part of my life
And without you,
Nothing has felt the same since.
I sometimes get scared about who I am or why I exist.
I sometimes ponder the point of living
If you're not here to see it with me.

The small glimmer of light that keeps me going
Is your immortality,
Knowing that I am here to honor your memory
With my thoughts, my smiles, and my tears
As I tremble silently and write this.

You will forever be the best part of my life
Long after the stars leave the sky.
You will forever be
The missing part of my heart.

I am almost certain
This pain would end
If I could just see you
One last time,
But speaking to you in my head
And making amends
Seems like the closest thing to closure
I can have in this life.

Believe me when I say:
The adoration I have for you,
I transmit into the cosmos each day.
I will forever love you
With every part of my aching bones.
And I have a feeling I'm not alone.
I just know.

yin and yang

Do not ask life to slow down for you
Because it won't.
Life will continue to do what it does best,
Providing you with unexpected blessings
Yet consequentially removing all your strength.
Life will make your dreams come true
Before taking back some hope;
It will throw you into a well
Before lifting you out with rope.
But what would life be
Without the yin and the yang?
The lemon tart hidden in a sweet meringue?
The gasping for air before the helping hand?
The tireless tug-of-war that emerges again and again?
Life would not be life if everything was simple.
The highs awaiting you wouldn't be worth it.
Take it all in.
The bitter
And the sweet.
Life will never apologize
For its unpredictability.

Your heart just doesn't beat the same. I know. Tears don't flow when you need them to the most. You'll stare at pictures of yourself before the loss, and it doesn't even feel like you're looking at the same person anymore. You would do anything to smile that way again. Life is not just broken. Life does not exist. Dissociation is clouding your vision and there is nothing you can do to stop it. Your memory is fading. The way you speak is changing. Looking after yourself feels like a luxury instead of a necessity, one you cannot afford. You are overcome with damaging thoughts and the taste of regret, drenched in this spiral of helplessness that never seems to end. Your body no longer feels like your home. You're navigating this battlefield alone. Grief has completely rewired the workings of your mind. The passions which set your soul alight are thrown onto the backburner as you indulge in those temporary pleasures for the night. You are feeling the walls of a disease-infested cave, reaching for that helping hand to guide you; but you're too scared to take the first step. You are a broken soul in search of something to make you feel a little less broken, but you don't know where to begin or if you should even try. You are terrified of the vulnerability that comes with the light, and you would much rather sit in darkness than risk being burned by going outside. But listen to me: you must take that step. Don't think about what comes next. If your body feels too weak, crawl. If your limbs are frozen, roll. Do anything but stall. By choosing to sit in the dark among the scattered shards of your heart, you will remain trapped. Any outcome is better than that. Don't let your growth be overshadowed by fear. You have so much more to witness, my dear. You have more to live for than you think.

I wonder if my tears reconcile after falling down my cheek.

I wonder if they dance together before disappearing into nothingness.

pot of gold

Life, you are pain,
But you are also the smell of the thankful grass
After a full day of rain.
Life, you really can sting,
But at times you are the brightest sunrise
Right before the day begins.
Life, you hurt;
You pour salt onto the wounds,
And sometimes it feels
Like something I cannot survive through.
But somehow, despite the lack of light,
It only takes seven faded colors in the sky
For a smile to wipe my face,
For me to feel thankful
To be alive.

That moment in the grocery store aisle three years ago when you slipped and dropped everything in your arms felt like it was the end of your existence at the time. With cheeks flushed, you looked around, and you could feel everybody laughing at you in their mind. You were embarrassed and ashamed; and so, you retreated to your car to cry alone. Nothing in that moment could have calmed you down or reassured you from your own hurtful thoughts.

But even a moment as mortifying as that one disappeared. It might have taken a day or a week of avoiding the store, but those who witnessed your fall were occupied with their own problems, their own responsibilities. You could soon after walk through that same aisle and shop for groceries like nothing ever happened. In hindsight, such moments are actually insignificant. But that's the difficult thing, isn't it? At the time, it feels like your entire world has come crashing down and those moments become all you can think about. But now when you reflect on that time, you reflect less on what others thought about you and more on the important things like the loved ones who were in your life or the partner you had by your side. You will reflect on who you were shopping for, what clothing style you wore; you may reminisce about a warm memory that happened later that day like singing in the kitchen with your sister while mixing buttercream frosting for your homemade cake. You will look back at this stage of your life the same way. You will wake up one morning and stop hating yourself for something you cannot control, a feeling that was never yours to hold. Each second, this feeling is passing by: a small moment in time which will one day be reflected upon with gentle eyes.

Sometimes, even breathing is especially difficult. A normal bodily function can be the most treacherous of tasks. And you don't have a reason as to why. On some days, all it takes is being looked at the wrong way to collapse into tears. And on others, you can hold onto pain better than anyone, disguising your torment until you explode into your pillow at the end of the night. You will have those days when you grow frustrated with the moon's patience as you eagerly await that natural reset. But this fresh start you seek will appear. The dancing stream of red and yellow on the horizon signifies a new mindset, a clean slate. Another chance to try again. You will be blessed with the gift of searching for rare gems sparkling between the tall grass once more, to breathe in fresh air your lungs failed to before. To smile instead of cry at the events of the previous day. To show life that you will never take it for granted, no matter what comes your way. You owe it to yourself to inhale as deeply as you can and hold your breath. You owe it to yourself to enjoy your presence. On the good days. The bad. And the in-between. Despite almost losing the ability to breathe, you are still here. And the possibilities are just as endless as you can believe.

To My Pillow,

I promise in the morning you will be nice and dry. But right now, I need your company, even just for the night. I promise to hold you close while I dream of a kinder life. Please don't ever think I take you for granted. You have saved my screams from being heard, soaked my tears after months of hurt, hugged me back while I left this world. You are my fluffy lifelong friend who comforts my cheek, my softest strength when I am weak. I am indebted to you for eternity.

daisies, birth years, and platinum tears

When the soul is in need of some clarity, there are answers to be found at the cemetery. Strolling through one with respectful intent is a truly transformative experience. In this open space occupied by flowers, ashes, and tombstones for miles, there is an epiphany that arises. The stillness forces you to reflect on what is important, the names of those loved and lost engraved in granite headstones. These were once people like you and me, with memories, and families, and minds filled with curiosity and beauty. We are not eternal in these bodies and this somber realization grants us the greatest lesson, a necessary reality: the emotions we feel are nothing short of temporary. Our worries, our concerns, these are all fleeting. And so, we must appreciate life for everything that it is to find true peace and come to terms with our shared mortality.

Sunshine and blue skies,
I know you're waiting for me
On the other side.

There hasn't been one day painful enough
That I haven't been able to heal from.
I speak about heartbreak and its ability to peel back my layers,
But I'm more resilient than I give myself credit for.
I am here in spite of the people who tried to break me,
The circumstances that tested me,
And the negativity spilling from the mouths of those who dislike me.
My emotionality is not to be confused for someone who is weak
Because I will walk through fire with peeling skin
And still remain standing.

oak tree

These tears of mine, they will not just fall.
They will birth seeds.
They will plant trees.
They will nurture a garden of flowers
Waiting to sprout.
They will seep into the Earth's soil
And nourish the roots of the oak tree
Which sits on top of the mountain,
Silent and lonely.
These tears of mine will not dissipate
And be forgotten;
They will birth what is to come next.
Let these tears symbolize the growth of myself,
The tightening grip of the roots around life's neck.
The predecessor to the challenges yet to come.
The ones I will fight until they are won.

You will not be forever consumed by this feeling of helplessness.
It will get better.

It always gets better.

Love yourself
as you
learn

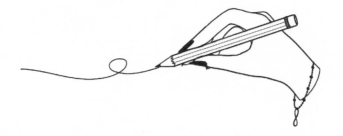

playful heart

A child will stumble many times
Before finding their balance
And just because your years on this Earth
Have been longer than theirs,
You justify speaking to yourself
With words that are callous.

You were once this child
Who tasted everything for the first time
And saw colors with a fresh pair of eyes,
And just because you can now drive and work a 9 to 5,
You find it an excuse to neglect your childhood side.

Please never forget
The resilient spirit you were
At the age of ten
Who laughed as you fell
And continued to try
Over and over again.

Speak to yourself as you would a young soul
Trying to regain their balance
Because you would never pass judgment
Or laugh at their efforts,
So why should your body be any different?

You are fragments of everything you have ever tried and failed. But darling, you are also everything you have tried that has set your soul alight and made the stars look in envy as you shined so bright. You are a beautiful combination of triumphs and shortfalls making your way through the Universe, trying with all your soul to piece together the reasons you are here for.

try, try again

The first time probably won't be a charm,
Just like the second or third time around,
But if you count your worth
On the amount of times it takes to learn something new,
You will only be doing yourself a disservice
And falling to the back of the queue.

Nobody is naturally born with the knowledge
To fly planes and operate on hearts,
But these people are equipped with the willingness to learn,
The undying passion, and their talent which takes them far.

Please try to be a little less critical of yourself
Because you are a soul exposed to the newness
Of these small parts of the world,
And when you eventually grow to be old,
You will have stories of success to be told
Alongside the failure you endured
Because you chose to be bold.

Nobody in this world has existed without learning in some form or another, so why do you place so much pressure on yourself while you do? The expectations to become fluent in a new skill, a new way of thinking, and a new way of behaving are eroding your core as you compare yourself to the person you were only yesterday. My dear, you are improving each and every day. Little by little. The change may be insignificant in your eyes. It may even be immeasurable. But it is happening. Each morning you are waking up as a more enriched version of yourself. As long as you are willing to expand your views, your body will be right there to help you. This new mindset you wish to master will soon become you. These miniscule anxieties you hold inside are vaporizing at the sun's emergence each day; the moonlight glistening in your eye is a reminder that you are doing okay. Fear lingers over the heads of those who haven't seen progress for fear they aren't on the right track. But despite this, you must persist. You must believe: believe that the new habits you practice in your waking moments are working, the bad addiction you have yet to break is weakening. Believe that your mind is the strongest asset one can have and it is on your side. Believe in your body's capability to fight for what is right. Keep going. Even on those days when you feel your progress is non-existent: those are the days you must especially push through to maintain that momentum. And your breakthrough will come. It may float on the horizon tomorrow morning. It may be a decade in the making. You may be pleasantly surprised by its timing or less than impressed. But one day, you will look back in admiration of those times when you persevered regardless. And you will grow to be content with your tremendous progress, all because you continued to believe in yourself.

You will fall down more times than you can count,
But you will apologize to
No one.

break the suspense

It's going to be messy.
You're going to take two steps forward
And three steps back.
You will grow to be angry at yourself
And the things you think you lack.
You are going to buckle down
And try even harder,
And there will always be that unexpected obstacle
Right around the corner.

But you must learn to be acquainted
Being met by the unexpected.
Turn the corner,
Even if the unknown awaits your fate,
Otherwise you delay the inevitable for another day
And create a hurricane of stress in its place.

You'll need to find a way
To tackle your concerns anyway,
So you may as well start today.
You will be surprised at the strength within you
That rises to the surface.
You will be shocked at your ability
To turn fear into progress.

Don't regret the mistakes, the embarrassment flushed across your cheeks, the crippling uncertainty, the ongoing anxiety, the fidgety nights spent overthinking into insanity. Each and every single one of your thoughts, whether right or wrong, have helped shape you into the best version of yourself. Life is an ongoing trial and error; you don't always need to have it together.

Rejection will take you places that acceptance won't.

the long road

Progress will sometimes feel like
Trying to fit a square block into a round hole,
Struggling to walk after a minor fall,
Taking the scenic route to find out it's busier than the main road.
Progress will sometimes feel like one step forward
And ten steps back
While you sit and think about what you lack
And question why you cannot move forward
As quickly as envisioned in your head.
Progress is taking out your shirt from the clothes dryer
To find it covered in lint.
It is cleaning your car to come back to it dirty
Because some teenagers thought it was funny to egg it.

Progress is the agony of not progressing
And forever stressing and second-guessing.
Progress by nature is not smooth sailing.
Progress is the art of moving yet waiting.
It is the practice of learning to be patient
And believing in the growth of the fruits of your labor.

Repeat after me: I will be gentle with myself. I am not perfect. This pressure I'm placing on myself is hurting. I must let go of this mindset. I must be kinder to myself. I am more than these expectations. And I am not any less if I do not achieve them.

When you learn to embrace imperfection,
you ease the weight of expectation.

Failure is, and always will be, unavoidable. Despite this, its impending visit shakes people to their core even though they have already experienced it many times before. How ironic the fear of failure when our greatest lessons have emerged from its presence, our accomplishments met with spells of amnesia and regret. Failure dims our motivation, triggers loss, and invokes emotional pain – it is a shot to the ego that most just aren't willing to take. But its positive side also shines bright during the difficult moments: those minor victories where you finally achieve a task you've fallen short of many times over, the unexplainable rush of confidence which would not have otherwise existed if it weren't for those trying emotions; learned lessons that will forever assist you in the future, the gratitude that your vision has now become clearer.

They say people only regret the chances they didn't take, so play your hand with confidence. If you lose, so be it. It won't be forever. Nurture the confidence within yourself to accept that no matter how many games you play, you're eventually going to win that one, because you will. It really only takes one. One moment in time. One change in circumstance to pave the way. One person who decided they were going to leave their fear of failure behind: someone who decided to give the world everything they've got.

That person can be you. All you have to do is shoot your shot.

The biggest triumph of your life is one "mistake" away.

lady luck

Roll the dice
And tell me twice
That life is simply
A game of luck,
A disillusioned façade
We hope to win
Yet forever blindly
Hide behind.
We roll the dice
Countless times,
Chasing doubles
Or the number nine.
We cross our fingers,
Cross our toes.
We sit back
And do nothing
Except hope
With unfavorable odds.
Lady Luck,
She desires the bold,
So instead of waiting
For your numbers to roll,
Pick a side,
Grab a marker,
And write your own.

it begins with you

We are taught to empower others and lift their spirits, to shower them with bouquets of respect, admiration, and bright yellow compliments. But we fail to appreciate the importance of empowering ourselves, the necessity of simply being our own best friends. We tell ourselves we love ourselves yet take every chance we have to doubt ourselves. Do we truly believe our words or live in sweet denial, hoping these positive thoughts eventually transpire?

We should be aiming to refresh our mindset in ways we didn't know were possible. We must be willing to lay our thoughts on the table; we must be willing to risk it all. Each and every day, we should be setting small goals. Our passion to grow must be greater than our fear of the fall. We should feel intimidated by challenging phases such as lifestyle changes because if they scare us enough, we will feel moved to accomplish them instead of procrastinating. Learning to love oneself includes the self-care and small talks to nurture your self-esteem but it also involves the goal-setting, the sweating, and the completion of piled up tasks for weeks because you have that vision in your mind to thrive and succeed.

Self-love is knowing you deserve better and making those choices so you are one step closer to becoming the person you wish to be, regardless of what you must leave behind, regardless of what you must do differently.

You are going to look back at the very moment you tried something new with adoring eyes and you won't believe the progress that flashed before them in the nick of time.

To My Mistakes,

How I sometimes wish you didn't exist. How I wish I could avoid the embarrassment and the relentless trial and error that emerges from your presence. How I secretly hope for you to cease following me as a reminder of what I lack. If only you could hide in the corner instead of making me feel I am under attack. But I must remind myself of your place in this world, like a single planet among a galaxy of stars or the tall dancing lights that control the cars. You are misunderstood. You are mostly uncomfortable. But you are necessary. You are imperative to growth; you are the very reason the wheels can still turn. And as much as you bring the bad, you also bring the good. You will be there to bring me down to earth while I learn to master a healthier train of thought. You will hold my hand during those countless hours of practice for a skill I try to perfect. You are the bridge between what has been and what will come next. Your existence is the reason that life makes any shred of sense.

I am learning that each step into this pain is a lesson
I won't have to suffer again.

Walking away from harmful energy is not as easy as others make it out to be. Most of the time, you cannot just leave a person you're in love with, even if they are narcissistic and manipulative. You think about it a thousand times over until their sweet-talking nature lures you right back through the door. But darling, you must remember that you are the one in control. You may not have the heart to leave right now but that doesn't mean you won't. Start uncovering your worth. Learn how to sharpen your intuition and become your own support system. Prioritize yourself over their insincere love until your soul simply has enough. I know the thought of packing your bags and walking out the door seems impossible, and you feel you don't have it in you to leave, but this does not make you weak. These traits make you a loveable, forgiving, compassionate human being and the moment you channel these traits back into yourself is the moment you will be free of their toxicity.

You would never taunt a flower for trying to grow, so why do you treat yourself so?

We are taught to tread lightly in new territory,
To walk ever so softly
Across the old swaying bridge in the forest,
To hold onto the railings at an ice rink
Before finding our confidence.
How are we taught to tread lightly in most situations
Except the one that is most important?
It is our tired souls that are trampled on
And abused without a second look
For we overestimate our ability
To hold ourselves together sometimes,
Piling on demands and expectations
Until we, ourselves, break.
Maybe if we saw ourselves as an old swaying bridge,
We would walk a little more gently,
A little more softly.

Nobody ever has it together one hundred percent.
Do not let their façade make you feel any different.

space

A word we associate with the stars above,
The key on our laptop,
That small pause between conversation,
And something in a box we need to fill up.

But space should be something
We regularly give ourselves:
A break
From the chaos
Of the everyday.

It should be a word
Associated with peace,
Serenity, self-love, and beauty.
An action filled with good intent,
Allowing steam from the heart
To vent freely.

Learn to breathe deeply.
Spread your arms wider
Than they have ever been.
Learn to ensure the space
You grant yourself
Is something you practice every day
And not simply a once in a blue moon soirée.

Learn to appreciate the fluidity of your thoughts, the fact they come and go. Learn to fall in love with your quirks for they are only yours. Acknowledge the lapses in your memory, and treat yourself gently. Learn to bask in the present and appreciate this moment. Embrace the cards you've been dealt and run with it.

doubts and diamonds

I have always been clumsy,
A little bit quirky.
I am the person who has an answer for everything
But will knock over the jug of water on the restaurant table.
I'm somebody who holds golden advice
But will accidentally hurt myself one too many times.
My laugh is guaranteed to be the loudest in the room,
But when times are tough, sheer strength I exude.
I am someone who has always felt utterly conflicted
With the idea of upholding that vision of perfection:
To pick a side, to choose a life
Where I must only be
One thing at a time.
So I finally took ownership of the fact
I can be that bubbly, warm-hearted girl
That you don't want to cross.
I can be the person who keeps her friends close
But prefers spending time alone.
I am a multifaceted being
Capable of feeling laughter, pain,
And everything in between –
And the great qualities I have within me
Are not exclusive
To the parts society wants me to be.

Take their advice – if not to learn from them, to take extra caution.

gold medal

You will feel like a failure
Many times over.
I promise you.
Life somehow finds a way
To make us feel inferior,
Regardless of how high
We build our confidence.
But just because you feel like one,
It does not mean you are.
Your essence cannot be
Diluted by society;
Only you can decide
Who you wish to be.
Feeling like a failure
Only shows that you care.
It is the greatest indication
That you are putting yourself out there.
You are exposing yourself
To more affliction and rejection,
But in doing so,
You are making your way closer
To that sweet moment of winning it all.
That gold medal, darling,
It is already yours.
You just need to believe it is first.

Their eyes should never be exposed to
the process, for you should surprise them
with your eventual success.

Your progress might be slow
But it's better than
Never moving forward at all.

Treat your every move
with confidentiality
because jealousy is
mostly disguised as
curiosity.

worker bee

By all means, allow your passion to ooze into your work, but never invite the shortcomings from your job to seep into your energy space. Your health is too sacred to be polluted with dollars, cents, and temporary mistakes.

You may love what you do. You may despise it. You may be a slow learner and hate yourself for being so. Your talents might not even be in the corporate world. You may constantly compare yourself with eyes of envy; you may be the biggest asset to your company. You may be celebrating a decade in your role; you may have been formally let go. The tension in your shoulders may persist in the office but disappear when you get home. You may be pairing your value with work when you really should not be doing so.

The economy will live on regardless of your shortcomings. Your abilities will probably be surpassed by someone new after you leave, and there will always be somebody out there with more desirable professional qualities, but please, take comfort in this reality. Your anxiety regarding work is a fleeting moment in a fast-paced world. Your concerns are trivial in the grand scheme of things. You are a human being with so much more to give. Your mistakes, your insecurities, the unrealistic pressures you place on yourself – these do not and will never determine your self-worth.

Acknowledge the importance of water and sunlight to a tree,
And consider why you should treat unhealthy habits any differently.

Practicing self-love after repeatedly being discouraged is more difficult than one can imagine. You will tumble too many times to count. You will wake up one morning proud of the person you have become and then run into someone who does something to make you feel insignificant again. You might trip over your words at work when speaking to a customer after spending every waking moment working on your stutter. You might bake a gorgeous cake and smear it with icing to find out the baking soda was in the sugar container. You may feel like a house of cards falling apart because of a small burst of wind. You could have accrued a world of progress to feel it come crashing down from one single thing.

Despite these occurrences which make you feel like the world is against you, please do not let them derail you. Don't feel discouraged by your progress; life is more imperfect than it is perfect. You are not unlucky. You are not hopeless. It takes time for habits to blossom. Learning to love yourself is an ongoing process, but a new aura will flourish like a flower in the sunshine if you allow it. The first step of hope is learning to rest; the next step is trusting the journey ahead.

untouched

The stovetop sizzles.
We burn our hand.
And we learn to never touch it again.

Words leave our mouths.
We are shown the consequence.
And we learn to tread with caution.

We think twice about a certain situation
When we are greeted with nothing but pain.
We close ourselves off from the world
When we are repeatedly left out in the cold.

But please,
Do not let the way people treat you turn you bitter.
Do not let their cruel actions become you.
Some are struggling with their own issues,
Projecting them onto you in hopes you'll catch on
And absorb their heavy moods.

Acknowledge, nod, and deflect.
You don't owe them anything else.
You can be mindful of the heat
Without having to burn your skin.

What if that one mistake
you wished you could undo
was the reason a blessing
was able to seep through?

There are infinite lessons to be learned from nature if you pay close enough attention. The dark, sticky cocoon left behind in exchange for a pair of wings. The persistent power of the ocean waves to erode the greatest of cliffs. The way humans treat the smallest of insects as insignificant when they are vital to the ecosystem. How a bee won't sting if you're saving it from drowning. The mercy that all creatures beg for when they know they are dying. There are the wolves that stick together no matter what, the alpha deciphering danger while leading the pack. We have the pouring rain to balance out the driest of days, the misfortunes to neutralize the lucky streaks. There is the warmth, the cold, the destruction, the rebirth. The natural catastrophes that tear apart land and souls, but also the blessing of solidarity to follow. It might sometimes feel unfair, but the cycle of life is anything but. Nature makes no mistakes. I hope you feel the same way about yourself.

Close your eyes and channel this:

The feeling of proudness within.

Not for any other particular reason, but for the fact that you are here and breathing.

Remember this feeling the next time you seek healing.

The fresh veil of the new day reveals lessons scattered on the concrete pathway.

Learn to withhold the apologies that leave your mouth.

They have their place. They can wait. The more you apologize, especially for things which are out of your control, you are telling the people around you that you feel unworthy of occupying space.

Do not apologize for standing in your own lane while somebody intrusively walks your way. You should not feel guilty if you are lucky enough to reap the benefits of fate.

The word "sorry" should only be used sparingly.
It should not be the dominant word in your vocabulary.

You have just as much right to be here as anyone else. Your little clumsy moments are not a reason to apologize for. Do not dampen the opportunities presented to you in any shape or form.

You are learning.

You are living.

You can never make everyone happy as long as you are breathing.

Please be mindful that the apology was created for a reason and its overuse will only leave you feeling helpless and weakened.

Some people exhibit rudeness and impatience towards a beginner,
Failing to remember they were new to something too, once.
If someone attempts to crush your spirit because you are still learning,
Just remember that their empathy is something they have yet to master
And that is not a reflection of you in the slightest.

learning curve

Indulge in the unpredictability of the learning curve.
Acknowledge its sharp highs and drastic declines:
The progress made that falls apart the very next day
And the feeling of countless hours in vain.
But also, take comfort in the fact
That your entire life can change
Just like that.
After a decline comes the biggest spike of your life,
The day when everything you've learned fuses together
To lift you into the sky.
The learning curve, it does not consistently climb.
It is a tangled web of shortfalls and triumphs,
Which will reward you with the results
You've been working toward
In due time.

There is beauty in insecurity.

Answers in uncertainty.

Calmness in urgency.

Clarity in ambiguity.

There are positives to be found in everything.

You just have to read between the lines, darling.

Dear Self-Critical Individual,

Take it easy on yourself. Learn to rest. You talk about yourself in
ways you would never talk about them. How is your soul meant to
heal when you continually spill such hate into your bloodstream?
Your mind treats this as acceptable when it absolutely shouldn't be.
Your recovery is in the silence just as much as it is in the curling of
the words; the sentences you arrange from now on should sparkle in
shades of love, not hurt. You are a human being who is in the midst
of a learning process. You are seeing things you haven't seen before
and feeling things you haven't felt before. You are training your mind
to grasp another process while navigating new territory like a ship in
uncharted waters. You are experiencing the world through a new lens
and changing habits that you have tried for years to break. Breathe.
And speak gently towards yourself, for the words you emit will surely
reflect.

One day, you will hear a knock on the door after what feels like a lifetime of waiting: a sound that will echo throughout your home with undertones of hope and inspiration. This thumping on the door will symbolize everything you have ever worked for, a sign that it is finally time to reap the rewards.

However, this person at your doorstep will not be a stranger. This person will be someone quite familiar.

Standing on your porch will be the version of yourself that persisted and kept going. They will look content, their skin will be glowing, and they will hug you with all their strength. Your blood, sweat, and tears fueled their existence. You created this powerful entity simply from your persistence. From now on, they are your mirror image, guiding you onto whichever path you see fit.

You will have made it.
Darling, you will make it.

Love yourself
and
believe

palette of lessons

I am starting to accept
That I am a work in progress.
I am an artistic mess scribbled
With lines of thick lead,
My bones forever exposed
To this everlasting process.
The day we stop learning
And wanting to try
Is the day we lie breathless
In the valley of life.
What is the point in simply surviving
When we should be thriving?
We should be falling, and learning,
And crying, and fighting.
We should be embracing the scars on our bodies
And painting them with sparkles and glitter.
We should be refusing to erase our mistakes
And sketching over them in pencil much darker.
We must never allow the choices of our past
To come back and haunt us;
Instead, we should be grateful
For the lessons learned that have allowed us
To appreciate the faded lines left on the clean canvas:
Reminders of how far we have come
And the resilience that now resides in us.

Those times I stitched my skin together led me to this moment,
And it's in this moment I found who I was meant to be.
How can I regret the blood and the tears
When they led me where I was supposed to be?

Look in the mirror with appreciation for all that you are: a powerful energy, a tender heart. You are a vibrant soul living among the stars; you are an embodiment of priceless art.

To the Person I Was That I Outgrew,

I do not hate you. I need to forgive the fact that you were only navigating this world with a different pair of eyes, seeing and witnessing things for the first time. You were living with a different state of mind, and it is only now that I truly appreciate the meaning of hindsight. If I had the choice to do things differently, I'd be lying if I said I wouldn't. But I guess the reality is that even if I wanted to, I just couldn't. So, I forgive myself. I forgive myself for not knowing better. I forgive myself for allowing people to treat me as less than, and worst of all, treating myself even worse than them. I forgive myself for the mistakes I made, the endless stream of self-induced heartbreak. The things I did then, I would never do now. And I forgive the person I was all those years ago because I was only living what I thought was right at the time.

Never again will I
Tend to the garden
Beside me while
Neglecting the one
At my feet.

I simply needed to be reminded of my strength
To build myself back up again.
I learned to reflect,
To be content.
Now with everything I do, I do with a bounce in my step.
I forgive my past self for the mistakes they made.
I am no longer afraid of the challenges that await.

floating on clouds

Darling, carry your flesh with confidence.
Breathe as if you've been granted a second chance.
You should smile like the entire world
Is in the palm of your hands,
And stand like you're on the peak of
Mount Everest.
Immerse yourself in the beauty of life,
And delve into the undiscovered sides
Of nature, of landscapes,
Of the people you adore,
Those interesting landmarks
Which electrify and allure.
Don't let this world
Make you bitter,
Make you sour.
Continuing to live with positivity
And vibrancy –
That's your greatest power.

Every "flaw" you wish you could trade
Is a feature someone else wants in your place.
Each "imperfection" you wear on your skin is
A unique stamp of your very existence.
This journey is one that only you have lived through.
Nobody else can walk in your shoes.
Your curves and your hues
Are exclusive to you,
And these qualities you wish to trade
With somebody else
Are only of value
To you.

A sign of growth is being able to embrace the warmth or the cold without thinking of the other and what you're missing out on.

A moment still exists if a lens is not there to capture it.
Memories are still created
If a camera is not there to witness it.
These experiences will forever rest
In the depths of your subconscious,
And so, you should never underestimate the power
Of the human mind.
The fear of losing recollection may frighten you,
But what is truly scary
Is wasting a unique moment behind a screen
That you will only relive through the photograph
And not the memory itself.

Nothing holds the power to harden your heart. You are simply too strong for that. After all these years, you are still the same tender soul making your way through the world with forgiving eyes. The thoughts inside your mind you no longer hide; instead, your emotions are wildly amplified. You are living with empathy, with kindness, with grace, with passion. You are a free spirit in admiration of the magnificence around you. Your curiosity is contagious to those who have the pleasure of knowing you. Your essence has transitioned into one more forgiving, and your patience for life's shortfalls is rapidly flourishing. You are here, and you are breathing despite the challenges that tried to destroy you. Your resilience is something nobody can take from you.

You will not allow this world to turn you bitter.

Despite the suffering your heart has been through, it now only beats for you. Your strength, it radiates in all the little things you do. You're still trying to make small talk with friendly strangers, even if it makes you nervous. Your mornings are not always perfect, but you make an effort to live in the moment. You talk a little too much and wear your heart on your sleeve because you've begun to embrace, not hide your vulnerability. You know what it's like to be excruciatingly weak, and so you lift others up when they are crumbling on their knees. The vibrancy of your energy is incredibly unique. You are a gemstone sparkling unapologetically.

Your strength lies in the way you radiate kindness each and every day. Darling, you are an absolute force to be reckoned with.

Those who cannot hurt you
Will resort to exclusion,
Not realizing the reason
You're so content in the first place
Is because you don't fit in with them.

You are a calm body of water with the
sun's reflection glimmering on the surface
but also the storm at sea with ten-foot
waves crashing roughly.

ashes of life

Nature's resilience is unmatched;
Even the spark from a match is
No match for her comeback.
The rejuvenation of the greenery after a bushfire
Will bring a tear to anyone's eye:
The tiny plants pushing through the dirt,
The leaves growing in place of the burnt,
Ashes instead becoming symbols of life
With seeds bursting open as they continue to fight.
These are the signs
That you, too, can once again thrive
Despite the pain,
Despite the vicious flames,
Despite the circumstances
That tried to burn your spirit
And take it all away.

The wind will gently blow your way.
And if you listen closely enough, it will whisper your fate.

Your younger self would be looking on with proud eyes that you made it this far. They were watching five years ago when you nearly collapsed from exam stress but also when you persevered anyway and aced your midterms. They were there during the biggest heartbreak of your life and that entire phase you weren't sure you could survive. They were secretly on the sidelines cheering you on, wishing you well, hoping you'd thrive. They believed in you when nobody else did, and now they smile with a tear in their eye.

To the Doubts That Are Quiet for Now,

I know you remain dormant in my mind, waiting to erupt when I am at my most vulnerable. But knowing you are weaker than you used to be is all I wish for. I know there are going to be times when I stumble again, when I fall harder than I ever have before. But the difference is that now I am ready for it. I am ready to use what I have learned and what I've felt to fuel the comeback again. I've lived at rock bottom and climbed my way up. Nothing is capable of keeping me down. My arms are open and ready to tackle anything that is thrown at me. No obstacle can withstand my ferocity.

I guess they'll never understand
That their words are gasoline
And I am the flame,
And their efforts to silence me
Blew up in their face.

my validation

After growing in this body,
Learning in this body,
Suffering in this body
With calluses forming on my soul
From the strenuous work
And surviving ordeals
I never thought I could,
I would much rather take a chance on me
And what I can do
Because these struggles, these hardships
Are ones I have endured.
I have experienced firsthand my strength,
Resilience, tenacity, hunger.
I had to preserve every breath of oxygen
Before I went under.
These eyes of mine
Have remained kind
After experiencing things
That would make anyone cry.
I have made it to the other side.
I've made it out alive.
And because of that,
I would much rather
Take a chance on me
In this life.

Your presence threatens them
Because you're a mile ahead in the fast lane
While they sit in traffic
Hoping your brakes fail.

gold blood

It is important to know
Not everyone wants to see you grow.
There will be some threatened,
Some jealous, some scared;
There will be those frightened
You are out to take what's theirs.
They will see you achieve.
They will see you thrive.
They will watch from a distance,
Yet make no effort to be on your side.
Your success and blind envy
Sadly go hand in hand –
So keep moving forward,
Crown glistening in the sun
Because you are authentic,
You are vivacious,
And nothing they do
Can make you come undone.

Change for them and you've sold your soul.
There is no cost greater than losing your home.

"Slow down," they said.
I smiled. "Maybe you should keep up instead."

I found myself being in a situation where the more I accomplished and the more I created, curious eyes appeared from afar. But it was only soon after that I felt the ill-intent seeping from people nearby as they tried to mirror what I had done. A lifetime of perfecting my craft became a novelty for those attempting to stage me up. A circus of titles and falsified accomplishments in counterfeit colors became unstuck.

So, I believed. I believed in myself. I believed in the pain I endured to get to this point. I sought comfort in the unhealthy number of tears that painted my skin and how they danced alongside countless hours of missed sleep. I held faith in my passion which will forever burn vigorously within me. I realized that the more goals you kick, the more people try to discredit you. And they will just never win. Because your determination, your drive, your originality – that's what makes you different.

Sit down, and grab a pen – school is in session.

1. Inspiration and imitation are two different things.
2. You can fake confidence
3. But not the intent that comes from it.
4. People will know, people can see:
5. You can't hide inauthenticity.
6. Passion is vital and it must burn within.
7. You must do what you do for the right reasons,
8. Not from a place of wanting to compete
9. But because you can't live without it.
10. If your intent is to undermine, you'll never go far
11. Because just as Karma dictates:
12. What goes around, always comes back around.

I'll take my rough-around-the-edges originality
over your clean-cut carbon copy.

They will see you found your passion
And try to take it away from you.
When that day comes, sit back and enjoy the view.
They cannot learn your lessons, feel your hardships,
Absorb the agony from your near-death experiences.
They cannot peer into your mind
And steal unborn ideas like yesterday's news;
They cannot steal your limelight
When it was always meant for you.

You cannot cherry-pick success.
So let them try their best.

It all starts with self-belief.
With this crucial foundation,
You can accomplish any feat.

Coming into your own will feel like your body is drenched in gold.
It will feel like a lifetime of dirt draining from your pores.
The weight of their opinions will slide down your skin
While the warmth of your being radiates within.
You will feel contentment with the soul that you are:
A dancing fireball in a galaxy of stars.
In this body that has never once felt whole,
You will break free from the unknown.

This is the day your soul returns home.

The salty air
And gritty sand
Taught me contrast
And love
Can coexist:
The seaweed,
The ocean mist,
The seabird hovering
In search of fish.
This panorama of
Opal blue
And off-white hues
Showed me the
Importance of
Enjoying the view
While appreciating how
Such harmony
Effortlessly ensues.

Fight to live another day for the decadent gelato you'll taste on a beach in Italy on your once-in-a-lifetime holiday. Fight for the small dog who doesn't usually come up to strangers but licks your hand anyway. Fight for the collection of shameless stories you'll hear from a stranger who has nothing to lose and how those stories of caution will replay in your head when you most need them to. Fight for the small moments that may seem insignificant individually but hold the weight of the world when the flashbacks of your life begin to play slowly.

To the Galaxy Inside Me,

You are unforgiving and unpredictable as much as you are vibrant and spectacular. The outsiders will never understand the extent of the struggles I've faced and the mistakes I've made because these are my stories to tell, my stories to keep. The challenges I have overcome, I do not wear on my sleeve, instead I associate them with the stars in the galaxy. There exist mistakes the size of stars that have followed me around in my life, exploding into messes burning brightly enough for me to spectacle with sparkling eyes. I sometimes find myself staring in awe as they float among the blackness before fading into nothingness. These stars are the ultimate reminder that nothing is ever permanent.

The promise I make to myself is to constantly keep trying.
I owe it to the warrior inside to create a story worth telling.

To the Misunderstood Mountain in My Mind,

Your peaks will be climbed. They will be explored. Every effort will be made to understand the way your curves flow into icy lakes and how the moss grows on the rocks covering the landscape. I promise to love the dangerous slopes just as much as I love the glistening snow peaks. I will not condemn you after slicing my leg on my descent because you cannot help the way you were made. Instead, I will use the sparkling lake at my feet to wash my cut clean. Your complexity will be adored even if it may not be understood, and nobody will be allowed to judge the way my mountain looks because it is only mine to see.

You are the embodiment of strength. You kept going. You kept moving forward despite the disappointment, the betrayal, the sheer agony you experienced. You didn't know what was going to come next but you did it anyway.

That is strength.

Strength is the uncertainty that you could find yourself in better times or be drenched by the night but persevering anyway because you have that confidence in your ability to fight.

Watch me emerge from my cocoon with wings covered in jewels.

hush, hush

Your motivation comes and goes, and you find that speaking with others about your dreams and desires only leads to disappointment for they dismiss each and every goal. They tell you with soft words they believe in you over and over again, but doubts rest on the tip of their tongue when you disclose a new project. These people you hold close, you love them with all your heart and that will never change, but they cannot see the error of their ways. Although their behavior is unknowingly destructive, you must not allow your enthusiasm to be dampened. Speak about your desires sparingly, and allow the fruits of your labor to grow silently.

Only after you present them with a luscious bunch of fruit will they see you proved them wrong while they eat their words and lick the sweet taste of amazement with their tongue.

Some things are only meant to be shared once they are done.

Confidence is
realizing your
worth does
not reside in
the stranger's
mind.

shine

You are a gold ring, carelessly dropped in the mud and made to feel you lacked luster when all you really needed was a cloth and some water. With some simple care and attention, your glimmer is brought back to life.

They may have lost their sight, but you never lost your shine.

How priceless the feeling of doing something they never said you could. And the best part being that you did it for you.

.

thank you card

There's a thank you card in my mind
That I'm sending to everyone
Who ever doubted me,
Those who left me behind.
I'm slipping it in between their mouth, carefully,
Held by their lips ever so gently.
They can taste my achievements
Written in ink
And think
About the doubt they thought
They instilled in me
And how it came back as a reminder
Resting between their lips
That the only thing they accomplished
Is staining their tongue
With their own bitterness.

Every single mistake you've made,
Every decision you thought was in vain,
Every uncertainty which plagued your head
For days and months on end
Has led you to where you are supposed to be
Today.
These lessons will continually guide you onto the path
You are meant to take
And hold your hand
Along the way.

divine wilderness

Here I am, staring at myself
A little too long
In certain moments,
Pondering to myself
Why I don't think I'm worth it
Purely based on this physical body of mine
That has allowed me to live life
Intertwined
Among the trees and the leaves,
The kind-spirited animals I am lucky to meet.
Maybe I am more than this physical body;
I am a gentle soul that drifts toward love in any form.
And maybe the doubts I have in my mind
Are a distraction from the light I hold
In the palm of my hands,
The abundance of tenderness held
Right here
In my heart.

You can look in the mirror forever and never notice it, but there's a slight glow on the surface of your skin. It's something only those around you can see. The way you curl your lips above your gums when you're smiling and showing your teeth. A luminosity unable to be captured through photography. Your tranquil aura sparkles in colors of glacier blue and ultraviolet. Life isn't a race for you, sweet child. There is no competition. Your spirit is a treasured existence of lessons and gifts in fruitful abundance. You don't glance beside you with jealous eyes. You are in your own lane, passing time. The wonders of nature captivate you with their simplicity as you drift among them harmoniously. You are a carefree spirit with the waterfalls of the Earth flowing from your soul. You radiate happiness and patience towards those who need it more. You're living your truth, creating and sharing your passions with the world. Your uniqueness has everybody staring in awe. My dear, you are a trailblazer, and they will forever remember your name because the footsteps you're leaving behind are incapable of fading away.

are you ready?

Stitch the threads of belief through your soul.
Invite the needle of hope to pierce the vein of doubt
As it bleeds out,
Draining years of self-hate and love unfound.

You cannot look back now.

Your essence is held by magical thread.
Darling, you owe it to yourself
To fight for better days ahead.

You will soon bask in the beauty of blue skies and belief,
A paradise you are on the road to discovering.
Before you know it, you will be standing at its gate
Ready to be invited inside.

Are you ready for the ride of your life?

Thank you for joining me on this journey, and I hope you resonated with my poetry.

I wanted to finish this book by reinforcing that the spectrum of human emotions isn't something we should shy away from, nor is it something to apologize for. Please, take time to regularly take care of yourself, especially spiritually and emotionally.

Speak to yourself with tenderness every day. Radiate positive energy towards those around you. This doesn't necessarily mean you need to adopt a bubbly, excitable personality or change what you're about, but by shifting your mindset and fixating less on the tension around you, you'll develop a newfound appreciation for yourself. All the things you'd usually give attention to will fade away while you channel your energy into things like learning new skills, meeting new people, and experiencing the world with a more open mind.

Place less pressure on yourself. You're doing great.

Everything that is meant for you will come when it is ready to.